Creative Saxophone Duets

26 stylish duets for beginners

Kellie Santin

Cheryl Clark

OXFORD
UNIVERSITY PRESS

Dear Student,

Creative Saxophone Duets is a fabulous collection of 26 stylish duets that encourage beginner students to enjoy making music with other players both inside and outside of lessons. It is intended to be used alongside *Creative Saxophone* and the duets follow the pace and technical progression of that book. There are also helpful references to the corresponding chapters at the start of each piece.

All of the duets have their own play-along track included on the companion website. The tracks are recorded in two transpositions, one suitable for alto and the other for tenor saxophone and offer the player an authentic experience of performing within an ensemble.

Of course, this book also works on its own and is suitable for any E♭ or B♭ instrument including alto, tenor, soprano, and baritone saxophones, as well as clarinet and trumpet.

Thank you for choosing *Creative Saxophone Duets*. We wish you many hours of happy music making!

Kellie Santin Cheryl Clark

Contents

Title	Creative Sax Chapters	Page
Let's go	1–3	5
Equality of the saxes	1–3	5
Taking it to the limit	1–3	6
Blast from the past	1–3	6
Mind the gap	1–5	7
Two's company	1–5	7
Jet lag	1–5	8
Cutting edge	1–5	8
Craving calypso	1–8	9
It's an illusion	1–8	10
Elizabeth	1–10	11
Put on your red shoes	1–10	12
The happening thing	1–10	13
Secret agent shuffle	1–13	14
Anyone for tennis?	1–13	15
In the meantime	1–13	16
Empty cupboards	1–15	17
Moving right along	1–15	18
Squeaky clean	1–15	19
Never say never	1–18	20
Excess baggage	1–18	22
Cool bananas	1–20	24
Under cover	1–23	26
Hot off the press	1–23	28
Gone troppo	1–25	30
And the winner is . . .	1–25	32

A tuning note (F♯ for the alto and B for the tenor saxophone) can be found on the companion website.

Getting started

Playing along with the tracks

- Visit the Companion Website at **www.oup.com/creativesaxduets** to access and download the play-along tracks.
- The icon on the **left hand side** of the piece title tells you the piece number.
- Tune up using the tuning note located on the companion website. The tuning note is **F#** for the **alto saxophone** and **B♭** for the **tenor saxophone**.
- Both parts are played on the play-along tracks. The top line is found on the left channel, and the bottom line is found on the right channel.
- When you are confident at playing your part, pan left or right (using the balance control on your audio equipment) and mute the part that you are playing. In this way, you can play along with either part as a duet.
- Remember to listen closely to the count-in at the beginning of each tune.
- Count the rests accurately.
- Most importantly, HAVE A GREAT TIME!

Chapters 1–3

1 Let's go

Kellie Santin

Chapters 1–3

2 Equality of the saxes

Kellie Santin

Chapters 1–3

3 Taking it to the limit

Chapters 1–3

4 Blast from the past

Chapters 1–5

5 Mind the gap

Rock

Kellie Santin

Chapters 1–5

6 Two's company

Waltz

Kellie Santin

Chapters 1–5

7 Jet lag

Cheryl Clark

Moderately

Chapters 1–5

8 Cutting edge

Cheryl Clark

Fast Waltz

Chapters 1–8

9 Craving calypso

Latin

Kellie Santin

Chapters 1–8

10 It's an illusion

Chapters 1–10

11 Elizabeth

12 Put on your red shoes

Chapters 1–10

13 The happening thing

Rock

Cheryl Clark

Chapters 1–13

14 Secret agent shuffle

Chapters 1–13

15 Anyone for tennis?

Chapters 1–13

16 In the meantime

Chapters 1–15

17 Empty cupboards

Slow Blues

Kellie Santin

Chapters 1–15

18 Moving right along

Chapters 1–15

19 Squeaky clean

20 Never say never

21
mf
mf
25
1.
2.
p
p
29
mf
mf
(straight 8ths)
36
p
p
(straight 8ths)
f
f
43
mp
mp
(straight 8ths)

21 Excess baggage
Kellie Santin
Majestically
Swing
f
f
5
mp
mp
9
13
17
21
mf
mf

25
Majestically
29
f
f
Swing
33
mp
mp
37
41
mf
mf
45
ff
ff

22 Cool bananas

17
mp
mf
mf
mp
mf
mp
21
mp
mf
mf
mp
mf
25
f
f
29

Chapters 1–23

23 Under cover

Kellie Santin

21
mf
mf
f
f
25
f
f
29
mp
mp
33
37
41

24 Hot off the press

21
mp
mp
25
mf
f
29
f
33
f
37

25 Gone troppo

Fast Latin

Cheryl Clark

21
mf
mf
25
29
mp
mp
33
mf
mf
37
41
mf
f
mf (1st time)
f (2nd time)

Chapters 1–25

26 And the winner is . . .